CORK
THEN & NOW

TOM CRONIN

The History Press Ireland

First published 2012

The History Press Ireland
119 Lower Baggot Street
Dublin 2
Ireland
www.thehistorypress.ie

British Library Cataloguing in Publication Data.
A catalogue record for this book is available from the British Library.

ISBN 978 1 84588 725 4

Typesetting and origination by The History Press
Printed in India
Manufacturing managed by Jellyfish Print Solutions Ltd

CONTENTS

INTRODUCTION

Early History

The name 'Cork' derives from the Irish *Corcach Mór Mumhan*, which means the 'great marsh of Munster' and refers to the fact that the centre of Cork City is built on islands, surrounded by the River Lee, which were marshy and prone to episodes of flooding. The waterways between the islands were built over to form some of the main streets of present-day Cork. The oblong-like shape of the centre-city island, bounded by the north and south channels of the Lee gives Cork City much of its physical charm.

St Finbarre

Traditionally, St Finbarre, or Bairre, has been credited with the foundation of the monastery of Cork. Little is known with certainty about Bairre, as the extant 'lives' were composed long after his death, reputedly in the seventh century, and contain mythical and folkloric elements. Whatever conclusions are reached about the historicity or otherwise of St Finbarre, his name has been given to many places and institutions within the city, most notably to the splendid St Finbarre's Cathedral, which is built on part of the site of the early monastic foundation of Cork.

Medieval Cork

By the medieval period, Cork was a well established and thriving town. Custom returns from the thirteenth and fourteenth centuries show that Cork was regarded as the principal port of south-west Ireland. The main imports were wine, cloth and spices, while the principal exports were wool, grain, beef and other agricultural produce from the surrounding countryside.

Economic Developments

Cork's prosperity declined due to the Gaelic and Gaelicised Anglo-Norman resurgence of the mid-fourteenth century, and further set-backs were caused by the Black Death and then the turbulent years of the 1640s and '50s. However, the city began to recover from 1660 to 1700, and the eighteenth century witnessed a major expansion in the economy of Cork. Cork's prosperity in the eighteenth century was based mainly on the provisions trade. Salted beef, pork and butter were exported to the West Indies and were used by the British Navy. The unrivalled ability of Cork Harbour to shelter the biggest fleets assembled during the American War of Independence and, later, during the Napoleonic Wars was a major factor in the expansion of the provisions trade in Cork. Cork Butter Market, with its strict and rigorously enforced system of quality control, was world famous and became the largest butter market in the world for its time. The nineteenth century once again saw a decline in Cork's fortunes. The ending of the Napoleonic Wars was a major factor in the economic slump. Prices for agricultural produce declined to one-half of the wartime prices. Cork Harbour no longer regularly hosted fleets of the Royal Navy and this caused a major decline in the provisions trade. Further misery was to follow with the ravages caused by the Famine.

The Cork International Exhibition

By the late nineteenth century, Cork had begun to recover and in 1901, the then Lord Mayor of Cork, Edward Fitzgerald, proposed that Cork should stage an international industrial exhibition in 1902. The proposal was enthusiastically received by all sections of Cork society and planning for the exhibition soon began. The site chosen was an area of parkland between the Cork County Cricket Ground and Wellington Bridge, now renamed Thomas Davis Bridge. The plans for the exhibition were extraordinarily imaginative and ambitious. It promised to be by far the most spectacular exhibition ever hosted in Cork.

The grounds were laid out meticulously, with pavilions, kiosks, ornamental walks and tea houses. An enormous water chute and a switchback railway featured among the attractions. Exhibition halls were built and a house on the grounds called 'The Shrubberies' was renamed the Mansion House for the duration of the exhibition. The event attracted exhibitors from across the globe, displaying their industrial, agricultural and artistic wares. It opened in 1 May 1902, amid scenes of celebration and enthusiasm. Its success surpassed all expectations, attracting visitors from all over Ireland, Europe and beyond. After it officially closed on 1 November 1902, it was decided to stage a similar exhibition in 1903.

First World War

Support for the war was widespread in Cork. Many men volunteered for the army and organisations were set up to support the troops, the wounded and the families of those in the armed forces. However, as the war dragged on and casualties assumed horrific proportions, enthusiasm waned. Cork got a taste of the horrors of the war when the *Lusitania* was sunk off the Old Head of Kinsale on 8 May 1915. Members of the Cork City Corps of the Irish Volunteers occupied St Francis Hall on Sheares Street during the 1916 Rising but no actual violence occurred in the city, due partly to the efforts of Bishop Daniel Cohalan and Lord Mayor Thomas C. Butterfield. The feeling that Britain would renege on the promise of Home Rule and on the withdrawal of the Irish Parliamentary Party from Westminster were among the factors that led to the victory of Sinn Féin in the general election of 1918. The divisions between Nationalists and Unionists were to the fore again, as Ireland slid seemingly inexorably towards the War of Independence.

Recent History

The more recent history of Cork, from the War of Independence to the present, is dominated by a struggle against economic stagnation, as many of Cork's traditional industries went into decline and thousands of Corkmen were forced to seek employment abroad. The 1980s and '90s, however, saw a change in Cork's fortunes, as it saw the benefit of the 'Celtic Tiger' era. New hi-tech industries moved in, transforming it into a vibrant and cosmopolitan city. In 2005, Cork was named European Capital of Culture, and, despite the recent economic problems, it remains a city with an air of confidence and optimism for the future. *(Credit: www.corkpastandpresent.ie/history/ historyofcorkcity)*

OPERA HOUSE

THE OPERA HOUSE in Cork began its life as the 'Athenaeum', after the old Greek centres of culture and art. It was built by the trustees of the Royal Cork Institution at a cost of £6,000. Its architect, Sir John Benson, had been responsible for many of the architectural features of the city. It was built for the 'promotion of science, literature and the fine arts, and the diffusion of architectural knowledge'. However, despite the pomp and ceremony which accompanied its opening on 21 May 1855 (it was opened by the Lord Lieutenant of Ireland, Lord Carlisle), it soon became obvious that the building was unsuitable for its purpose, the acoustics being most unsatisfactory. Some noteworthy people who did appear on its stage were: Charles Dickens, who lectured twice in the old Athenaeum; Brian Dillon, who sang there at a Fenian concert, and Parnell, who spoke there at a meeting – it was on that occasion in fact, that he made his famous statement, 'No man has a right to fix the boundary of the march of a nation.' In 1873, it was remodelled and renamed the Munster Hall, but neither was that venture a success.

At this time. Cork's principle theatre was the Theatre Royal in George's Street, but this was taken over by the postal authorities, so a group of citizens, under the chairmanship of Mr John George McCarthy, formed the Great and Royal Opera House Co., and purchased Munster Hall. Mr C.J. Phipps of London was commissioned to redesign and re-equip the theatre, and on 17 September 1877, Cork's Opera House opened its doors to the public.

The new theatre began its long life with a visit from the immortal Sarah Bernhardt and her famous company. She came from America for this visit and, as the liner was late in arriving at Cobh, the company, costumes and effects were transferred to a tug which sailed up the river and tied up at the quay alongside the Opera House. Financially the new venture did not prove successful for the Great and Royal Opera House Co., and it wound up in 1888. Nevertheless, there was sufficient enthusiasm in the city for the theatre, and in the same year the Cork Opera House Co. was formed, with a capital of £12,000.

The beautiful old Cork Opera House burnt down on 13 December 1955 and construction of the today's building began with the laying of the foundation stone on 21 June 1963. *(Credit: www. corkoperahouse.ie/content/history)*

SCHOOL OF ART

THE INCREASING SIZE of cargo ships entering Cork meant that new quays were constructed to accommodate them further down the river, and the position of the Old Custom House became unsuitable. A new Custom House was built in 1810 and the old building fell into disuse. Several Cork philanthropic and educational bodies, such as the Royal Cork Institution and the Cork

Mechanics' Institute, applied to the government for the use of the building, but it was not until 1832 that the RCI was finally able to move its considerable library, scientific instruments and collection of sculpture casts into the old building.

For the following two decades, the Old Custom House became the centre of art and science education in the city. However, with the founding of Queen's College Cork in 1849, the RCI's useful life was effectively brought to an end, and that same year the Old Custom House was re-opened as a Government School of Design, one of a large number of such schools which were established throughout England, Ireland, Scotland and Wales at this time.

In 1884, through the patronage of William Horatio Crawford, a large extension was added to the School of Design, which was then renamed the Crawford School of Art. This extension and the original Custom House now form the Crawford Municipal Art Gallery.

WOODFORD, BOURNE

ONE OF THE most distinctive buildings in the centre of Cork City is situated at the junction of St Patrick's Street and Daunt's Square. This building now houses McDonald's but was, for over a century, the well-known premises of Woodford, Bourne & Co., grocers and wine merchants. The company can trace its origins back to a firm of wine merchants named Maziere & Sainthill, which was trading in Cork as early as 1750. Maziere & Sainthill had premises in Nelson's Place (the older name for Emmet Place).

Invalids PORT, Carefully Decanted off the Crust, **3/6** per Bottle

WOODFORD, BOURNE & CO. LTD**., 64 & 65, P**

An Old Established House noted now over a Century for the Ch

Brandy

FOUR

• ❖ ● ●

STAR

REGISTERED

GUARANTEED

14

YEARS OLD,

6/-

per Bottle

CK STREET, CORK,

lity of their supplies.

In the mid-nineteenth century, John Woodford had a grocery shop on the Grand Parade. Woodford died from an illness contracted while he was engaged in charitable work during the Famine. After his death, his widow married a Mr Bourne, who was an employee of Woodford's and thereafter the firm was known as Woodford, Bourne & Co. In 1869, Woodford, Bourne bought the stock of the wine merchant Richard Sainthill and expanded the business to include wines. An employee of the firm, James Adam Nicholson, an immigrant from England, eventually became sole owner and the firm remained in the hands of the Nicholson family for generations. The shop on St Patrick's Street was one of the best-stocked shops in the city and the firm also owned extensive warehouse premises on Sheares Street.

In the 1980s, the shop was converted to a fast-food outlet named 'Mandy's' and the premises was taken over by McDonald's in the mid-1980s. *(Credit: www.corkpastandpresent. ie/places/stpatricksstreet/selectedplacesofinterest/ woodfordbournecoltd/)*

HIBERNIAN BANK

IN 1825 A number of experienced London bankers, seeing an opening for a
Joint Stock Bank in Ireland on the lines of those so successfully in operation in
Scotland, established the Provincial Bank of Ireland, which opened its first branch in Cork in
that year. Conducted with enterprise and prudence, its success was soon assured. In the days
when much of our wheat supply was home grown and all our flour home manufactured, it had
the largest share of the business of the corn merchants and millers of the city and district, and
when times changed it adapted itself to the new state of things and continued to enjoy its fair
share of business. The Hibernian Bank building was remodelled in 1945 to a design by Levie,
architect of 11 South Mall, Cork. *(Credit:* Alphabetical Directory City and Suburbs of Cork
1875-76 and Irish Architectural Archive, www.dia.ie/architects/view/1024#tab_biography)

MUNSTER AND LEINSTER BANK

IN 1908, A competition was held, entrants to which were asked to submit designs for the proposed Head Office of the new Munster & Leinster Bank. From eleven competitors (all Irish), the plan of Mr Arthur Hill was declared the winner by an Independent assessor, Mr C.C. Ashlin.

The first steps in the implementation of Mr Hill's scheme were undertaken in 1910. Adjoining houses were demolished, and the new building was constructed so that a substantial portion of the old premises would be untouched. The design was conceived around a number of Breccia marble columns, of which Hill had some knowledge. Six of these pillars were procured in 1853 for St Paul's Cathedral in London. They were intended to carry the organ but were never used. Hill's design, however, needed eight pillars, so the Breccia quarries, which had been closed for decades, were reopened and two huge masses of marble were quarried to provide the essential missing columns. These pillars are surmounted by alabaster caps of rich Ionic design, containing a wealth

of foliage and cherubs. They stand on plinths of a rich brown Devonshire marble. The corner piers acting as responds are formed of arnialli marble with molded caps of alabaster to correspond. In order to represent the interest of Irish craftsmanship, polished Midleton red marble, Connemara green marble and jet-black Kilkenny marble were used in the complementing floor and wall patterns.

Massive doors of deep-tone mahogany with bevelled glass panelling give the bank an imposing air. The loftiness of ceiling and dome springs on one with surprise. The contrast in height between vestibule and latter hall is truly an architectural 'touch of the wand'. The hall is 38ft square and the height from floor to dome is 46ft.

The dome is formed in a circle, two-thirds of which is executed in artistic plastering, whilst the remainder is of dulled glass. The four pendentives of the dome are delightful studies in the highest craft of plaster working and these were done by Richard Sisk.

At a height of 12ft from the floor and above the counter runs a magnificent balcony of embossed bronze. In the hall are four handsome mahogany tables designed by Hill and built by Cork tradesmen in the workshops of Sisk & Sons.

The total cost of the building reached £50,006 9s 8d.
(Credit: Cork Library)

MURPHY'S
BREWERY

THE MURPHY FAMILY'S association with Cork started some time between 1709 and 1711, with the arrival of Nicholas O'Murphy in Carrigrohane, west of Cork City. Nicholas's son Jeremiah then moved closer to Cork, leasing land in Bishopstown. Jeremiah married Mary Anne Redmond and they had two sons, Daniel and Jeremiah. The eldest son, Daniel, became a farmer, while Jeremiah moved into Cork City and entered the leather trade.

In 1854, James J. Murphy and his brothers purchased the buildings of the Cork Foundling Hospital and built a brewery on the site. The brewery eventually became know as the Lady's Well Brewery as it is situated adjacent to a famous 'Holy Well' and water source that had become a

MURPHY'S FAMOUS STOUT

*From experience I can strongly recommend
Messrs. J.J. Murphy's Stout.*

Eugene Sandow

JAMES. J. MURPHY & Cº LTD
STOUT & PORTER BREWERS. CORK.

famous place of devotion during Penal Times. In 1856, James J. Murphy and his brothers founded James J. Murphy & Co. and began brewing.

In 1889, a malt house for the brewery was constructed at a cost of £4,640 and was 'built and arranged on the newest principle and fitted throughout with the latest appliances known to modern science'. Today the Malthouse is one of the most famous Cork landmarks and continues to function as offices for Murphy's. The Murphy Brewery celebrates over 150 years of brewing, and the now legendary stout is sold in over forty countries and recognised worldwide as a superior brand. James J. Murphy would be proud. *(Credit: http://www.murphys.com/index.php)*

BEAMISH AND CRAWFORD

THE BEAMISH AND Crawford brewery was founded when William Beamish and William Crawford purchased an existing brewery (from Edward Allen) on a site in Cramer's lane that had been used for brewing since at least 1650 (and possibly as early as 1500). Beamish and Crawford's 'Cork Porter Brewery' prospered, and by 1805 it had become the largest brewery in Ireland and the third largest in the then United Kingdom as a whole. In 1805, its output was 100,000 barrels per annum – up from 12,000 barrels in 1792. It remained the largest brewery in Ireland until overtaken by Guinness in 1833.

In 1865, the brewery underwent a modernisation programme and was completely revamped at a cost of £100,000. Alfred Barnard, a noted brewing and distilling historian, remarked in his book *Noted Breweries of Great Britain & Ireland* in 1889 that, 'The business of Beamish &

Crawford in Cork is a very old one dating as far back as the seventeenth century and it is said to be the most ancient porter brewery in Ireland.'

The company went public in 1901, issuing a share capital of £480,000. Further expansion was aided by the acquisition of a number of local breweries in the early 1900s. In 1962, it was purchased by the Canadian brewing firm Carling O'Keefe Ltd, who embarked on a modernisation programme at the brewery. In 1987, Elders IXL purchased Canadian Breweries (incorporating Carling O'Keefe). In 1995, Elders sold the brewery to Scottish & Newcastle.

With the 2008 takeover of Scottish and Newcastle, the brewery passed into the hands of its main Cork-based rival, Heineken International.

In December 2008 it was announced that the Beamish & Crawford brewery was to close in March 2009 with the loss of 120 jobs. The products currently brewed there will henceforth be produced at the nearby Heineken Brewery (previously Murphy's), with about forty of the Beamish staff moving to Heineken.

The brewery buildings (including the Tudor-fronted 'counting house') are still situated in the heart of Cork's medieval city, close to the site of the city's South Gate. *(Credit: www.wikipedia.org/ wiki/Beamish_and_crawford)*

IMPERIAL HOTEL

THOSE FIRST GUESTS arrived at the Imperial Hotel in 1816, when all of Europe was still talking about the Battle of Waterloo and its two outstanding personalities, Napoleon and Wellington. This long saga of the Napoleonic Wars had been important to Cork, not only as a matter of news but as an affair of big business.

The city was then noted throughout Europe for its butter market and from 1800 onwards the butter merchants grew prosperous. The Committee of Merchants, who directed all this activity with remarkable finesse and enterprise, were anxious for a commodious building in which to transact their affairs, to read the foreign newspapers and to drink claret in convivial company. In 1813, they commissioned the young Cork architect Thomas Deane to design and build the commercial rooms on the South Mall. The dignified façade of Deane's building stands virtually unchanged today and forms the front portion and main entrance of the Imperial Hotel.

It was in 1816 that the merchants requested that Deane extend the original building along Pembroke Street to serve as a hotel and coach-yard.

The choice of the South Mall was an inspired one. Just twenty years before it had been one of the many open channels of water on which modem Cork is built, like Grand Parade and Patrick Street. In time, the

Mall became one of the most gracious avenues in the city, with its lines of trees and its long sweep of red-brick Georgian houses interspersed with banks built in the classical style from local limestone.

The Imperial Hotel is very much part of life of Cork from 1816 onwards and its coach-yard in Pembroke Street witnessed all the excitement of the arrival of the stage coaches; the pageantry of the coach master, the guard, the hostlers, the blacksmith, the steaming horses, the baggage men, and the travellers for whom the hotel was journey's end.

In its 174 years of hospitality, the Imperial has welcomed many notable guests coming by coach and by car: the great Irish painter Daniel Macuse stayed here; the novelist William Makepeace took tea in the lounge with Fr Theobald Mathew, the apostle of Temperence; Charles Dickens gave a reading in the Clarence room; Daniel O'Connell addressed a glittering assemblage there, and Liszt gave a piano recital. *(Credit: Imperial Hotel Cork)*

QUEEN'S OLD CASTLE

FOR WELL OVER a hundred years, the Queen's Old Castle department store was one of the best-known shops in Cork City. The site of the store – lately occupied by the Zavvi music store, which closed in March 2009, and the catalogue retailer Argos – is one of the most historic and interesting sites in the city centre. Confusingly, it was originally the site of the King's Castle, one of the two fortresses guarding the entrance to the medieval port of Cork. The original Queen's Castle was further to the north, near present-day Castle Street and Cornmarket Street. Both castles are shown on the Pacata Hibernia map of Cork from the late sixteenth century. The King's Castle is on the south of the Watergate on the map, while the original Queen's Castle is clearly

marked north of the Watergate. The King's Castle got its name from a charter of Prince John (later King of England) of around 1189, which ordered that a fortification be made for his use in the city.

The earliest documentary evidence that definitely identifies the location of the castle is from 1608, when a grant to a member of the Fitzgerald family mentions the 'Kinges castle, on the south side of the Key [present-day Castle Street] neere and upon the walls of the Cittie of Corck'. Earlier references to the castle in the historical sources are confused and contradictory. Despite this, historians feel that the King's Castle was built in 1206, as the Annals of Inisfallen for that year refer to a castle in Cork that was built by the foreigners. The Annals of Inisfallen for 1230 record the destruction of a stone castle in Cork and this was almost certainly the King's Castle. It had been rebuilt by 1232, when it was in the custody of Peter de Rival. Despite the confusion in the historical record there is a consensus among historians that the castle functioned until the late fifteenth century. There is also evidence that it was used as a gaol in medieval times. Later references indicate that the castle was in a ruinous condition after the late 1500s. Following an order from James I in 1609, all or part of the castle was demolished and the County Courthouse was built on part of the site.

PROVINCIAL BANK

No. 97 SOUTH MALL was constructed as the
Provincial Bank of Ireland to the design of William
G. Murray, architect. The builder was Alexander
Deane, reputed to be an uncle of Sir Thomas Deane,
the well-known Cork architect. The building was
completed in 1865 for a cost reported variously
between £15,000 and £20,000.

The most striking features of the building are
the two magnificent decorative façades, behind
which is a hierarchy of spaces ranged around three
sides of the central banking hall. There are many
external carvings on the upper levels of the façade,
including the coats of arms of various Irish cities and
representations of industry and commerce, symbolic
of the sources of business of the original Provincial
Bank of Ireland.

The banking hall rises through the full height of
the building, terminating in a high vaulted ceiling

THE IRISH ASSURANCE

and the roof lantern light. There is extensive decorative plasterwork to the ceiling, cornices, the walls and the original door surrounds. The vaulted ceiling is of particular interest.

In the late 1960s, Provincial became part of the Allied Irish Banks amalgamation and it was occupied by Allied Irish Banks until 30 June 2000, when it was acquired by Thomas Crosbie Holdings Ltd as its corporate headquarters. *(Credit: Thomas Crosbie Holdings Ltd)*

CORK CITY CLUB

ONE OF THE most beautiful buildings on the Grand Parade stands on its
south-west corner and now houses the Bank of Scotland (Ireland). Formerly
it was the Cork City Club and dates back to the early 1800s, although it was
extensively renovated in 1860. A post office stood on the site of the Cork City
Club in the mid-eighteenth century. In Smith's map of 1750, the south-west
section of the Grand Parade is named Post Office Quay.

   The post office moved to Caroline Street in the early 1800s and a clubhouse, at
first called Daly's Club, occupied the site of the old post office. *Holden's Triennial
Directory 1805, 1806 and 1807* lists Daly's Club, and Pigot's Directory of 1824
describes the premises in the following terms, 'Daly's club house, on the Grand
Parade, is a plain extensive building, in which are handsome reading rooms, card
rooms, &c, for the use of its members.'

   Daly's Club House was a gentlemen's club with facilities for the members to
play cards, play billiards, read newspapers, and take refreshments. In the early
nineteenth century there were three gentlemen's clubs in Cork: Daly's Club
House; the Cork County Club on the South Mall; and the Grand Parade Club at
the corner of Tuckey Street and the Grand Parade. In 1860, Daly's Club and the
Grand Parade Club merged and the new club was named the Cork City Club. It
was housed in the premises of the former Daly's Club House. The building was

extensively refurbished in 1860 with designs drawn by Sir John Benson and Robert Walker. The builder employed to carry out the renovations was Daniel Barrett. The *Cork Constitution* of 29 August 1860 described the renovations, 'In excellent taste and the coup d'oeil [a glance that takes in a comprehensive view] of the whole as seen from the South Mall will be at once, chaste, simple, and effective.'

In 1952, Cork City Club and Cork County Club were amalgamated and decided to use the premises of the County Club on the South Mall. The City Club premises were put up for auction and bought by the Legion of Mary, a lay Catholic organisation, for £9,120 on 13 March 1952. The other bidders at the auction were J.J. Creed, a solicitor from Macroom acting on behalf of an unnamed client, and J. Carr, acting on behalf of Cork County Council. The building was renamed Dún Mhuire and became the headquarters of the Legion in the diocese of Cork. In later years the Legion of Mary vacated the building which then housed ICC Bank for a time before becoming a branch of the Bank of Scotland (Ireland).

With its pristine white frontage and its distinctive architecture, the former Cork City Club is still an ornament on the newly redeveloped Grand Parade. *(Credit: www.corkpastandpresent.ie/places/ grandparade/corkcityclub/)*

GENERAL POST OFFICE

THE OLIVER PLUNKETT Street section of the GPO in Cork stands on the site of an old theatre called the Theatre Royal. The Pembroke Street section is on the site of an old branch of the Cork Savings Bank. The Theatre Royal was founded by the actor Spranger Barry and was opened in 1760. It was modelled on the Crow Street Theatre in Dublin, where Barry had previously worked. This theatre was destroyed by a fire on 1 April 1840. In 1853 the theatre was rebuilt and the name of Theatre Royal was retained. During the 1860s, the theatre was extensively refurbished under the direction of the outstanding architect Sir John Benson. The refurbished theatre was officially opened on 26 December 1867. In 1875, the theatre was sold to the postal service and the new GPO was opened in 1877. *(Credit: www.corkpastandpresent.ie/places/stpatricksstreet/ selectedbuildings/generalpostoffice/)*

MONUMENT

THE NATIONAL MONUMENT on the Grand Parade in Cork was unveiled on St Patrick's Day 1906. The monument commemorates the rebellions of 1798, 1803, 1848 and 1867. Fr Kavanagh, OSF, unveiled the monument as bands from Cork City and from the county towns played 'Who fears to speak of '98?' D.J. Coakley, a well-known architect, designed the monument.

Patrick Meade, the Mayor of Cork, laid the foundation stone of the monument on 2 October 1898. The spot chosen for the monument, at the junction of the Grand Parade and South Mall, had formerly been occupied by a statue of George II. King George was astride a yellow horse at this location and this gave rise to the Gaelic street name of – 'An Sraid Cappail Buí'.

The *Cork Examiner* described the National Monument in the following terms:
'The style of the monument is in the early Irish Gothic. At the base there are four steps, with a boldly-moulded plinth. Over this arm two cusped panels on each face, the spandrils being filled in with carving, and these are surmounted by a richly carved and moulded coping, which forms the base to the monument.' *(Credit: www.corkpastandpresent.ie/places/grandparade/nationalmonument/)*

ST MARY'S POPES QUAY

THE DOMINICANS WERE established in Cork in 1229, thanks to a nobleman of Welsh origin, Philip Barry. Their priory was built outside the city walls, on a small green island in the south-west suburb, which they dedicated to the Mother of God. From its insular position it came to be known as Sancta Maria de Insula – St Mary's of the Isle. A little bridge with a gatehouse or tower secured an approach.

For the first 300 years the Dominicans did their work unmolested, and Cork priory produced many notable Dominicans, some of whom served as bishops at home and on the continent. The next 300 years, however, were a different matter and they were subjected to much persecution from the ruling Protestant authorities, culminating in the accession of William of Orange in 1690, when new persecution laws were enacted against bishops and friars all over the country and the Dominicans were driven from their ancient priory, never to regain possession of it.

The last prior was Fr Peter O'Garavain. St Mary's of the Isle was given to the Mayor of Cork for a residence. In later times it was called the Great House of St Dominic's, and became the town house of the Earl of Inchiquin. The site was used in the nineteenth century for a distillery known as 'St Dominic's Distillery'. Today part of the site is occupied by the Sisters of Mercy and bears again the name 'St Mary's of the Isle'.

Due to the extraordinary energy of Fr Batt Russell, who was born in Cork in 1799, a new St Mary's church and priory were built. It was designed by Kearns Deane (1806-1847) and the foundation stone was laid in 1832. Keane, a talented and generous Protestant, gave his services free of charge, and the gratitude of the Dominicans is expressed in a marble tablet in the most frequented of the church porches. 'The Dominican Community of Cork inscribe this stone as testimony of their gratitude to Kearns Deane Esq., architect, who with unexampled generosity and public spirit designed this building and directed the progress of its erection, 1832'. On Sunday 20 October 1839 the church was blessed and opened for public worship. In the congregation was Daniel O'Connell, 'The Liberator'. *(Credit: www.dominicans.ie/friars/communities/cork/history.html)*

ST ANNE'S, SHANDON

THE CHURCH OF St Anne's in Shandon is one of Cork's oldest buildings. Built in 1722, it is almost 300 years old and is the oldest religious site in continuous use in the city.

The present church, which replaced an earlier building, is built from rubble red sandstone and ashlar limestone. The structure comprises a Victorian timber barrel-vaulted ceiling, barley twist communion rail and an early eighteenth-century balcony sitting on four carved Iconic columns.

There are also five stained-glass windows, beautifully colourful and of the highest craftsmanship. Of special interest are the MacDonald window (in memory of Mary MacDonald) and the Hubert McGoldrick's oval St Luke's window.

The font, dated 1629, was rescued from the original church, which was destroyed in the 1690 Siege of Cork.

By the early 1770s, the church had become a parish in its own right and the Revd Arthur Hyde was appointed as its first rector in 1772 (great-great-grandfather of the first President of Ireland).

The famous eight bells in the tower were cast by Rudhalls of Gloucester in 1750 and were installed in 1752. They weigh over 6 tonnes and each bear an original inscription. *(Credit: St Anne's Shandon Historical Society)*

BUTTER MARKET, FIRKIN CRANE

PART OF THIS building is a museum dealing with the development of Cork as a trading centre in the 1700s and the development of the Cork Butter Exchange, which became the largest butter market in the world.

The Firkin Crane building was designed by Sir John Benson and opened in 1855. The building is a unique rotunda, which formed part of Cork's original Butter Exchange, with the former butter market buildings in the Shandon area.

The butter trade originating from Cork City in the eighteenth and nineteenth centuries stretched to Great Britain, Europe, North America, the Caribbean, and the West Indies. Indeed, the building's name derives from Danish words pertaining to measures of butter. 'Firkin' is a Danish word meaning 'quarter barrel' and in former times these firkins or casks were tarred and weighed on a balance known as a crane. The main routes to the market were called 'butter roads'. Farmers from as far away as Kerry came to sell their butter. D.L. Kelleher describes the butter merchants in his travel book *The Glamour of Cork* (1919), 'At 7a.m., the merchants are up and to their offices in Mallow Lane. They are an easy, oily folk, fair skinned, as though the softness of butter was blended in their faces.'

The butter went through a strict process of testing before it was categorised into five types, 'first' being the best and 'bishop' being the worst. This made Cork butter very popular, as the strict quality control meant that people knew exactly what type of butter they were buying.

The Firkin Crane is also of archaeological significance, as it was constructed on the site of medieval Shandon Castle. This site was occupied by the Dominicans, who had a chapel and convent here from 1784 until 1840.

When the butter market closed in 1924, James Daly & Sons occupied the building until the 1970s, when they moved their margarine manufacturing business to new premises.

The Firkin Crane was completely destroyed by fire in 1982. It reopened in 1992 and is now a bustling centre for dance of all kinds. With four dance studios and two performance spaces, it is a unique building for dance in Ireland. Large-scale performances run throughout the year, along with a range of regular classes and workshops across a spectrum of dance styles. *(Credit: www.corkbutter.museum/about and www.askaboutireland.ie/learning-zone/primary-students/ looking-at-places/cork-city/moments-in-cork-city-hist/cork-butter-exchange/)*

NORTH CATHEDRAL

THE CATHEDRAL OF St Mary & St Anne, known locally as the North Cathedral, is located at the top of Shandon Street, in one of the most historic areas of Cork. The cathedral is the principal church of the diocese of Cork & Ross and is the place where major diocesan celebrations take place. It was dedicated in 1808 and celebrated its bicentenary in 2008.

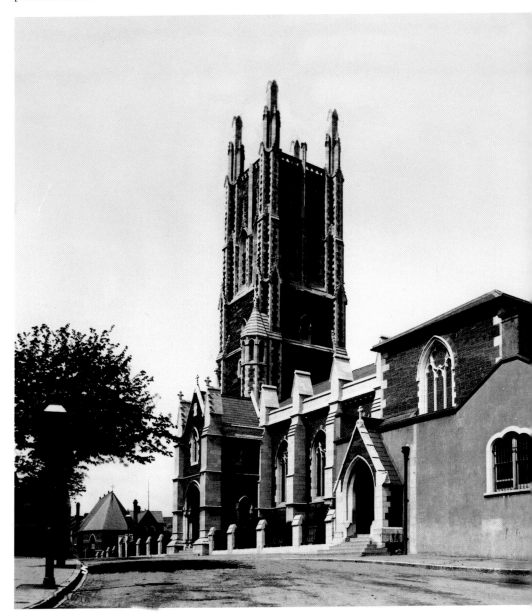

In 1820, a fire of mysterious origin caused near-catastrophe to St Mary's. In those days, municipal fire brigades were as yet unknown; each factory maintained its own fire-fighting unit. The cathedral might have been completely destroyed but for the prompt arrival of the fire brigades of Messrs Hewitt, distillers, Watercourse Road, and of Messrs Wise, distillers, North Mall.

A notice in the *Cork Morning Intelligence* on 10 June 1820 conveyed the thanks of the parishioners to Messrs Hewitt and Wise. It was added that the damage to the cathedral had been estimated at £2,000. A meeting of the citizens was summoned to devise ways and means of reconstruction.

In 1964, an extension to the sanctuary area was undertaken and the internal layout was reorganised. A sanctuary tower was constructed, rising to a height of 80ft to complement the western tower.

In 1996, major repairs and renovation were again required. The cathedral closed for the duration of the work. The tower was completely renovated, the roof re-slated, the gothic ceiling repaired and external stonework repointed. The sanctuary also underwent a major refurbishment and the interior was generally upgraded. Parishioners and clergy, people of the diocese and beyond raised more than £3.5 million during that period.

ST FINBARR'S

LEGEND HAS IT that St Finbarr was the son of Amergin, whose tribe was descended from Eochaidh Muidmheadoin, brother of the King of Munster. Amergin settled in the territory of Muskerry, in the county of Cork, where he obtained an inheritance and land at a place called Achaidh Durbchon, near the spot afterwards known as Gougane Barra, at the sources of the River Lee. He was chief smith to Tighernach, King of the Hy Eachach of Munster, and he married a young woman of the king's household. As this was in defiance of the king's wishes, the couple was summoned before him and he sentenced them to be burned alive. A storm of thunder and lightning, with heavy rain, prevented the decree from being carried out. This was regarded as a divine interposition and they were set free.

A child was born from this union and they returned to Gougane Barra, where the boy was baptised Luan, or Lochan. When he was seven years old, three clerics of Munster, returning from a pilgrimage to Leinster, happened to stop at the house of Amergin. They admired the boy for the grace of the Holy Spirit that seemed to them to shine in his face, and were allowed to take him away to be educated. He studied at a place called Sliabh Muinchill, where, as was usual at the time, he was tonsured and had his name changed. The cleric who cut his hair is said to have observed, 'Fair [finn] is the hair [barra] of Luan.' 'Let this be his name,' said another, 'Barr Finn, or Finn Barr.'

William Burges was appointed architect for a new cathedral in 1862, after a competition in which there were sixty-three entries. Among the requirements of the competition was that the cost of the building should not exceed £15,000, and Burges was criticised by other architects because the cost of the towers, spires and carving was not included in his estimate. In the end some £100,000 was spent on the building.

During the building work, nine stone-carved heads (or 'voussoirs') dating to the twelfth century were found embedded in the walls of the medieval tower. It is thought that these were either from an earlier cathedral or part of the Augustinian house of St John the Evangelist, which subsequently became known as 'Gill Abbey'. Its site was some 400m west of the cathedral and was possibly within the old monastic precinct of St Finbarre's. These artefacts are of huge significance, not least because they may have been carved by the same stonemasons who worked on Cormac's Chapel in Cashel. It is hoped to have some of these on public display in the cathedral in 2012. *(Credit: www.stfinbarres.wordpress.com/history/ and www. cathedral.cork.anglican.org/index.php/history1/ the_medieval_cathedral1)*

HUGUENOT CHURCH

THE AREA AROUND French Church Street and Carey's Lane is known as the Huguenot Quarter of Cork City. The Huguenots were French Protestants who fled from religious persecution during the seventeenth century. When the Edict of Nantes (1598), which had granted religious freedom to French Protestants, was revoked in 1685, many Huguenots chose to leave France, with about 5,000 of them settling in Ireland. The community of Huguenots in Cork City never numbered much beyond 300. Another, smaller wave of Huguenot *émigrés* followed in the latter half of the eighteenth century, until the French Revolution finally ended the denial of civil and religious liberties to Huguenots.

On coming to Ireland, some of the Huguenots conformed to the principles of the Church of Ireland, while others chose to worship in independent or non-conformist churches of their own. The non-conformist Huguenots in Cork bought some property in 1712 and established a church between the modern-day French Church Street and Carey's Lane. An adjacent graveyard was later established. The Huguenots worshipped at the church in French Church Street until 1813, when declining numbers caused its closure. The original building was demolished in 1845 and a new church was erected by the Primitive Wesleyan Methodists.

The Primitive Wesleyan Methodists had been using the old church since 1819 and continued to use the new church until 1897. Many of the Huguenots remaining attended worship in churches of the Church of Ireland.

The Huguenots became prominent in the commercial and civic life of the city soon after their arrival in Cork. From the seventeenth to the nineteenth centuries, many Huguenots served as Sheriffs and Mayors of Cork. In the commercial field, the Huguenots were prominent in trading and textile manufacture, while as craftsmen they were noted as goldsmiths and silversmiths. Some of the best-known Huguenot surnames in Cork included: Besnard, Pick, Lavit/Lafitte, Perrier, Godsell, Quarry, Hardy, Malet, Perdrian and Delacour. *(Credit: www.corkpastandpresent.ie/mapsimages/ corkphotographs/corkcameraclubhistoricalphotos/huguenotchurch/)*

WATERWORKS

THE BUILDINGS WHICH stand at the waterworks site today date from the 1800s and 1900s, but water has been supplied to the city of Cork from the site since the 1760s.

By the first half of the nineteenth century, it was felt that the water supply to the city required upgrading. The population of the city was increasing rapidly and new suburbs developing on the city's north side could not benefit from the existing system as they were above the water basins. In addition, it was considered that the use of wooden pipes and untreated, unfiltered water was outdated. Thomas Wicksteed, one of the most respected water engineers of the time and engineer of the East London Waterworks, was commissioned to report on the existing services and make recommendations for a new scheme.

In 1854, the Pipe Water Company instructed John Benson to make a survey of the existing waterworks. By February 1857, Benson had prepared a plan for a new waterworks, based on Wicksteed's earlier recommendations. Work began with the laying of new cast-iron mains pipes in 1857 and continued for a number of years. By February 1859 these new water pipes had reached the military barracks on the Old Youghal Road. By this time, the Pipe Water Company had been taken over by Cork Corporation, who remain in charge of the municipal water supply to this day.

In the 1860s, three further beam engines were acquired, as the Cornish beam engine was not providing sufficient power. New buildings had to be constructed to house these engines, as well as a boiler house and a coal store.

Between 1902 and 1907, Benson's scheme was altered when the Cornish beam engine was replaced with three triple-extension engines made by Combe & Barbour of Belfast. Two Lancashire boilers were installed to supply the steam to power these engines. These are the engines and boilers seen at the site today.

The original engine house of Benson's 1860s scheme had to be altered and enlarged to house these engines and its original appearance was significantly changed. However, the original chimney stack was retained. *(Credit: Lifetime Labs, Cork Waterworks)*

LORD MAYOR'S PAVILION

THE LORD MAYOR'S PAVILION in Fitzgerald's Park has been carefully restored by Cork City Council and was officially re-opened on 14 June 2011 by the Lord Mayor and the British Ambassador.

The building, which was built in 1902 in the Arts and Crafts tradition to welcome visiting dignitaries to the Cork International Exhibition, has had its roof, walls and windows sensitively repaired as part of an essential works contract, overseen by the City Architect's Department on behalf of the Recreation Amenity & Emergency Services Directorate.

Project architect Neil Purkiss praised the contractors, Murphy & O'Sullivan, for their dedication to the works through a particularly harsh winter. He added, 'This contract involved a limited scope of badly needed external works, necessary to stabilise and future-proof this very significant and unique architectural gem. Although timber-framed and modestly conceived, it reminds us all of the extraordinarily successful development of the Mardyke area in 1901, in which a large number of temporary buildings were constructed to accommodate the Cork International Exhibition.'

The neighbouring Cork Public Museum houses a collection of fascinating images of the buildings and structures that made up the Exhibition in Fitzgerald's Park, including a Victorian roller coaster known as a 'switch-back railway', a water slide on the river and the magnificent Industrial Exhibition Hall, overlooking a water fountain that remains in the park today.

Fitzgerald's Park was named after Lord Mayor Edward Fitzgerald, a builder by trade, who was the driving force behind the exhibition and whose grandson Jack Fitzgerald was present at the official opening.

The building, which now includes a generous south-facing terrace, will continue to be used by the Park Wardens to promote nature conservancy to visiting groups of schoolchildren and has also been proposed as a versatile craft promotion and display centre for the artists of the city. *(Credit: www.corkcity.ie/services/architects/lordmayorspavilion/)*

UNIVERSITY
COLLEGE CORK

UCC WAS ESTABLISHED in 1845 as one of three Queen's Colleges at Cork, Galway and Belfast. The site chosen for the college is particularly appropriate, given its connection with the patron saint of Cork, St Finbarr. It is believed his monastery and school stood on the bank of the River Lee, which runs through the lower grounds of the university. The university's motto is, 'Where Finbarr Taught, Let Munster Learn.'

On 7 November 1849, Queen's College Cork opened its doors to a privileged section of the youth of Munster (115 students in that first session, 1849/50) after a glittering inaugural ceremony in the Aula Maxima, which, the newspapers remarked, already looked mellow though just completed, and which is still the symbolic and ceremonial heart of the college.

The limestone buildings of the main quadrangle were designed by the gifted architectural partnership of Thomas Deane and Benjamin Woodword. The style has been variously described as perpendicular Gothic, Tudor Gothic or Victorian Gothic. The north wing of the main quadrangle houses UCC's unique collection of ogham stones, thought to be burial stones or boundary markers. The inscriptions are the earliest written source of the Irish language and the oldest recordings of Irish personal names, dating back to the mid-fifth and late seventh centuries.

Sir Robert Kane, distinguished industrial scientist and first president of the college, passionately defended the 'mixed education' non-denominational principle against the charge of 'godlessness', emphasising the built-in provisions for respecting religious beliefs and even for promoting religious practice.

Courses were offered in the faculties of arts (comprising literature and science), medicine, law and in the schools of engineering (civil and mechanical) and agriculture. Students paid college fees, but also class fees, directly to their professors and lecturers. Popular lecturers became wealthy men!

For the first thirty years, men dominated college life. The first female students were admitted to Queen's College, Cork in the academic year 1885/6. Until the early years of the twentieth century, all academic staff were male. However, by 1910, Cork was the first Irish college to appoint a female professor, Mary Ryan, Professor of Romance Languages.

One of the university's most famous lecturers was Professor George Boole (lecturer between 1849 and 1864), the great mathematician, who is best remembered for his development of Boolean algebra, without which modern computer science would be impossible.

University College, Cork is now one of four constituent universities of the federal National University of Ireland. (Credit: University College Cork, Library Department)

GAOL

IN THE DAYS of the Queen's and Royal Universities, the number of students attending the Cork College did not exceed 200-300, but with the foundation of the National University the numbers have increased year by year, today exceeding 1,000. When one considers the large increase in the student population and the demand for more diversified scientific training, it must be admitted that the time is ripe for increased building, if University College, Cork is to hold its place in the academic world.

It was realised that the present grounds could not accommodate the new buildings without overcrowding and therefore impairing the beauty of the college. The site of Cork Gaol was the obvious solution of this difficulty. Consequently, the president approached the powers-that-be and, largely through the active personal interest taken in the matter by An Taoiseach, a portion of the gaol was allotted for the future extension of University College.

This portion had a frontage of 260ft on the College Road, an average depth of 125ft and an area of almost one acre. It was a valuable building site, abutting on the College Road and contiguous to the Physics-Chemistry building.

The space also included the graves of the men who were executed by the British during the 1916/21 fight for independence. A Cork Memorial Committee collected about £2,000 and ordered a suitable monument designed by the well-known Cork sculptor Mr Séamus Murphy. *(Credit: P. Coffey, ME)*

FRANCIS WISE HOUSE

THE HOUSE AT the junction of the North Mall and Wise's Hill was the residence of the distiller Francis Wise, after whose family the hill is named. The North Mall distillery was established on Reilly's Marsh around 1779, and by 1802 the Wise brothers were running the firm. Cork Distillers Co. bought it in 1867. The North Mall distillery was described in detail in Alfred Barnard's *The Whisky Distilleries of the United Kingdom*, published in 1887. A fire severely damaged the distillery in 1920. The site of the old distillery is now jointly owned by University College Cork and the Mercy University Hospital. *(Credit: www.corkpastandpresent.ie/mapsimages/ corkphotographs/corkcameraclubhistoricalphotos/ franciswisehouse)*

EYE AND EAR HOSPITAL

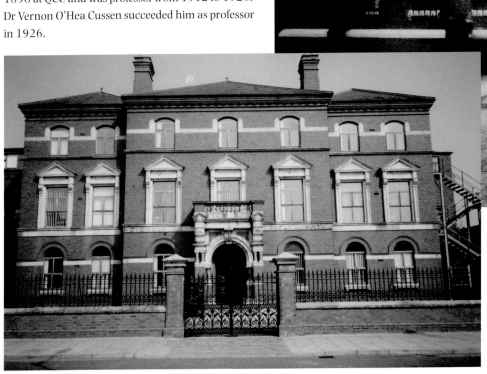

THE CORK OPHTHALMIC HOSPITAL was founded in October 1868 in Nile Street (Sheares Street), mainly through the efforts of Dr H. McNaughton Jones, who was its first physician. Prof. C.Y. Pearson tells us, 'he was surgeon in the old Eye, Ear and Throat Hospital in Nile Street. His efforts there in giving voluntary teaching to any student who wished to attend were indefatigable. He held special evening clinics and taught us the uses of the ophthalmoscope, auriscope and laryngoscope.'

In the first eleven years of its existence, over 2,000 intern and 20,000 extern patients were treated. Dr Arthur Sandford succeeded Dr Jones in 1882; he was appointed lecturer in Ophthalmology and Otology in 1890 at QCC and was professor from 1912 to 1926. Dr Vernon O'Hea Cussen succeeded him as professor in 1926.

In 1897, the Eye, Ear and Throat Hospital was opened on the Western Road, and the patients transferred from Nile Street to the present building. Alderman P.H. Meade, Mayor of Cork, presided at the opening ceremony – a very large and representative meeting of citizens – and was presented with a gold key to open the hospital by Lady Bandon. There were twenty-five beds in the old hospital in Nile Street and forty-six beds in the present building. Mr Cooper had been Hon. Treasurer since 1882. Since 1897, the work of the hospital has steadily increased in every department and today is only limited by the hospital's current size. *(Credit: Professor Wilson, author, The Iron Throat)*

VICTORIA HOSPITAL

THE VICTORIA HOSPITAL was founded as 'The County and City of Cork Hospital for Women and Children', which was opened on Union Quay on 4 September 1874. It was moved to 46 Pope's Quay on 31 October 1876 and to its present site on 16 September 1885. In 1901, its name was changed to 'The Victoria Hospital for Women and Children'. Male patients were first admitted in 1914. On 17 August 1914, the hospital was registered under the Companies Acts, 1908 and 1913, under the name of 'The Victoria Hospital, Cork (Incorporated)'.

In 1885, the old South Infirmary buildings were leased from the Trustees of the South Infirmary. After extensive rebuilding, they were opened as part of the hospital on Wednesday 16 September, on which date all the patients from Pope's Quay were successfully transferred.

Owing to the serious financial position of the hospital, 'The Wonderland Bazaar' was held in 1896. As a result of its efforts, the sum of £1,654 was raised, which nearly liquidated the bank overdraft.

The South Infirmary-Victoria University Hospital Ltd came into existence on 1 January 1988, as a result of the amalgamation of the South Charitable Infirmary and the Victoria Hospital. Prior to that date both hospitals operated as separate entities from their inception dates – the South Charitable Infirmary and County Hospital from 1761 and the Victoria Hospital from 1874. *(Credit: www.sivuh.ie/aboutus/history.html)*

THE BLARNEY STONE

BLARNEY CASTLE, AS viewed by the visitor today, is the third building to have been erected on this site. The first, in the tenth century, was a wooden structure. Around 1210 this was replaced by a stone structure which had the entrance some 20ft above the ground on the north face. In 1446, the third castle was built by Dermot McCarthy, King of Munster, of which the keep still remains standing.

The lower walls are 15ft, built with an angle tower by the McCarthys of Muskerry. It was subsequently occupied at one time by Cormac McCarthy, King of Munster, who is said to have supplied 4,000 men from Munster to supplement

the forces of Robert the Bruce at the Battle of Bannockburn in 1314. Legend has it that the latter king gave half of the Stone of Scone to McCarthy in gratitude. This, now known as the Blarney Stone, was incorporated in the battlements, where it can now be kissed. *(Credit: www.blarneycastle. ie/pages/history)*

BLACKROCK CASTLE

THE ROCKY LIMESTONE outcrop on which Blackrock Castle sits today has been a site of fortification since the late sixteenth century. The original tower was built by the citizens of Cork in 1582 to guard the water approach to the city from pirates and other raiders. The tower also acted as a sentinel to guide shipping safely to and from the port. Indeed, the motto on the crest of Cork City is '*Statio Bene Fida Carinis*', meaning 'A Safe Harbour For Ships'.

Following the 1601 Battle of Kinsale against the Spanish, Lord-Deputy Mountjoy replaced the fort with a castle in 1604 but this was as much to protect himself from the citizens of Cork as from the Spanish.

The people of Cork, ever rebellious, were slow to acknowledge James I as their king. It was during this time that Haulbowline was fortified and James Fort was built in Kinsale. As well as being strong enough to mount artillery for the protection of Cork Harbour, the main tower of the castle had an outside diameter of 10.5m and a wall thickness of 2.2m – unusually thick for an Irish castle.

In 1608, James I returned control of the castle to Cork City. From now on the castle would meet the needs of the City Corporation and have less to do with the defence of Cork.

In 1722, the main tower was destroyed by fire and rebuilt by the citizens of Cork at a cost of £296. The castle was used by the corporation for banquets and convivial gatherings. Traditionally the Mayor of Cork is also the Admiral of the Harbour, and Blackrock Castle was the seat of the Admiralty Court until 1827, when a party after the Annual Banquet led to a fire that destroyed the castle once again. Under the direction of Mayor Thomas Dunscombe, the castle was rebuilt in 1829 at a cost of £1,000.

In the early twentieth century, Blackrock Castle was used as a meeting place for local organisations but had fallen into disrepair by 1930. In the 1960s it was acquired by a group of Cork businessmen for use as a bar, restaurant and more recently as commercial offices and even as a private residence. In 2001, the building was once again bought by Cork Corporation for IR£825,000.

The most recent work on the castle began in April 2002 with inspection and conservation of the remaining structures. On-site construction began in 2003, with roofing a major priority. During the works a policy of minimal intervention was adopted. This means that wherever possible, original structures would be preserved and incorporated into the new structure before the introduction of more modern materials. The recent conservation work has now been completed and the building has begun its new life as CIT Blackrock Castle Observatory, housing a Cork Institute of Technology research facility, a restaurant and bar and an award-winning state-of-the-art science exhibition. *(Credit: Blackrock Castle Trust)*

BLARNEY HOUSE

AT THE BEGINNING of the eighteenth century, during the reign of Queen Anne, Sir James St John Jefferyes built a Georgian gothic house up against the keep of Blarney Castle, as was the custom all over Ireland. At the same time the Jefferyes family laid out a landscaped garden known as the Rock Close, with a remarkable collection of massive boulders and rocks arranged around what seemed to have been druid remains from pre-historic times. Certainly, many of the

yew trees and evergreen oaks are extremely ancient. In 1820, the house was accidently destroyed by fire and the wings now form a picturesque adjunct to the keep, rearranged in the 1980s to give a better view of the keep. The Jefferyes family intermarried on 14 January 1846 with the Colthursts of Ardrum. Lady Colthurst decided to build the new castle in Scottish baronial style, south of the present keep. This was completed in 1874 and has been the family home ever since. *(Credit: www.blarneycastle. ie/pages/history)*

FOTA HOUSE

FOTA HOUSE WAS originally a modest two-storey hunting lodge belonging to the Smith Barry family. The family lived in Britain, coming to Ireland for fishing, shooting, hunting and yachting. In the 1820s, John Smith-Barry (1793-1837) decided to make Fota his home. He commissioned the great Irish architects Sir Richard Morrison and his son William Vitruvius Morrison to convert the hunting lodge into an elegant residence.

Initially it was proposed that the design should reflect the current fashion for Tudor revival, but a more elegant Regency style was ultimately executed. Two new wings were added and a handsome Doric portico made an elegant entrance. The interior was opened up with fine

scagliola columns, leading to a handsome stone staircase. The ceilings of the library and drawing room were decorated with great delicacy in the French style.

In 1872, the engineer Sir John Benson designed the beautiful billiards room and an extensive conservatory. In 1897, the conservatory was altered to become the present long gallery. The house has remained virtually unchanged since this time, and the visitor today has a privileged glimpse of the great craftsmanship that was to be found in Ireland in the eighteenth and nineteenth centuries.

The house has over seventy rooms, ranging in size from the more modest servant rooms to the large and beautifully proportioned principal rooms. The curious 'dummy' windows on the exterior of the building were added to enhance the aesthetic balance of the house. The style is classical throughout and the decor reflects continental trends in the gilt, marble work, painted ceilings and magnificent plaster detail throughout.

Since the re-opening of the house in 2009 after restoration, people can now visit its upper floors for the first time in many years. *(Credit: www.fotahouse.com)*

FRIENDS' MEETING HOUSE

THE QUAKERS, ALSO known as the Society of Friends have had an unbroken presence in Cork since the 1650s. The Meeting House shown in the photograph was built in 1833, replacing two former buildings on the same site, and was used for worship until 1939. After 1939 the building was used as a medical dispensary by the Southern Health Board. It is now a health centre administered by the Health Service Executive. A new Quaker meeting house was opened at Summerhill South in that year.

George Fox, who founded the Quakers, visited Cork in 1669. It was in Cork also that William Penn became a Quaker. Penn's family had extensive properties in Cork.

Many Cork Quakers were merchants and businessmen and were widely respected for their honesty and industry. During the nineteenth century the Beales, the Pikes, the Newsoms and other Quakers were among the most successful merchants and industrialists in Cork. During the Famine, the Cork Quakers, like other Friends around Ireland, opened soup kitchens in an attempt to alleviate the suffering caused by that dreadful catastrophe.

A fine history of the Quakers in Cork is Richard Harrison's *Cork City Quakers: A Brief History 1655-1939*, privately published by the author in 1991.

VICTORIA HOTEL

THE VICTORIA HOTEL was built in 1810 and retains much of its Victorian splendour, from the handsome marble exterior down to the brass rails and fixtures in its attractive cocktail bar. The hotel was frequented by European royalty and by numerous leading Irish politicians, including Charles Stuart Parnell. In the literary world, James Joyce recounts his stay in the Victoria Hotel in his novel *A Portrait of the Artist as a Young Man*. (Credit: www.diningpubs.com/restdisp. asp?restid=431)

METROPOLE HOTEL

ALTHOUGH MUSGRAVE IS now best known for its SuperValu/Centra and cash-and-carry operations, it has, during the course of its 125-year history, been involved in a diverse range of other commercial activities, including the coal business, hotels, laundry, bacon, sweets manufacturing, tea blending, shop fitting, construction and frozen foods.

Among Cork's famous landmarks, the Metropole Hotel was one of the best known of these other businesses and it is still going strong after over 100 years. What is less well known is that, for the first eighty years of its existence, the hotel formed an integral part of Musgrave. Indeed, it was largely the need to issue preference shares to fund the construction of the Metropole and the adjacent sweets factory that induced Musgrave Brothers to incorporate as a limited company in 1894.

At a board meeting of Musgrave Brothers held on 20 April 1896, the contract to build the hotel was awarded to John Delaney & Co. This company had already been awarded the contract to build a sweets factory for Musgrave Brothers at the rear of the King Street (now MacCurtain Street) site a year earlier.

The following month, Musgrave Brothers raised £8,625 from issuing fifteen hundred 6 per cent preference shares at £5 15s each. The offer was well received – in fact, it was oversubscribed by a massive thirteen times. This was only one of a number of preference-share issues by the company in the mid-1890s, with approximately £20,000 raised in total.

The Metropole was designed by architect Arthur Hill and built to the highest standards. Not only did the Metropole incorporate the height of late-nineteenth-century luxury, it also had one other feature which, while unusual from our modern viewpoint, was relatively common in those days. In keeping with Musgrave Brothers' refusal to deal in alcohol, the Metropole was a temperance or 'dry' hotel. This had practical as well as ethical advantages for the company, since the main customers of the Metropole in its early days were commercial travellers, including those employed by Musgrave Brothers or those doing business with the company. Accommodating them in an establishment without a liquor licence helped keep them on the straight and narrow. *(Credit: Musgrave Group SuperValu/ Centra, Metropole Hotel Cork)*

GRAND PARADE

THE GRAND PARADE is built over a channel of the Lee, like so many of the other streets in the centre of Cork City. The channel that later became the Grand Parade is shown in the earliest maps of Cork. In the late eighteenth century, Cork Corporation built culverts to carry the water for some of the channels of the Lee and built the streets over them. The channel had been completely filled in by the late 1780s.

The Grand Parade is the widest street in Cork. Its Irish name, Sráid an Chapaill Bhuí (the Street of the Yellow Horse), refers to the time when a statue of King George II on horseback stood near where the National Monument now stands. The statue was painted a golden yellow colour in 1781. It was knocked from its pedestal 1862 by persons unknown and Cork Corporation removed the entire structure later that year.

The Grand Parade and the area behind it to the west are among the most important archaeological sites in Cork. It is near to the earliest sites inhabited by the Hiberno-Norse settlers on the South Island near the South Gate Bridge. Archaeologists now think that what appears as one island in the 1545 map of Cork may, in Hiberno-Norse times, have been a series of

small islands separated by narrow channels. The small channels were filled in over time and by the sixteenth century the area looks like one island. Much of the area has yet to be excavated, but the excavations that have taken place indicate that the area has been inhabited since at least the twelfth century. Among the items found were pottery, textiles, nails, and wooden structures from houses. Many of the finds are on display at Cork Public Museum. *(Credit: www. corkpastandpresent.ie/places/grandparade/)*

ST PATRICK'S STREET

MOST AUTHORITIES AGREE that St Patrick's
Street was formed in 1783. It is not shown on
Rocque's map of 1774 but there are entries for
the street in Lucas's directory of 1787. During
the 1780s, many of the streets that now form the
city centre of Cork were formed by the spanning
of the river channels between the islands of the
Lee.

During the late eighteenth century and the
opening years of the nineteenth, the North and
South Main Streets still formed the commercial
hub of Cork City. It wasn't until the 1820s
that St Patrick's Street began to assume its
role as the principal commercial centre of the
city. A comparison of directory entries for St
Patrick's Street for 1810 and 1824 shows the
increasing commercial importance of the street.
The opening of the first St Patrick's Bridge in
1789 helped the development of the street
by providing an approach from the northern

suburbs. The revival of trade and commerce in Cork in the eighteenth century provided a great social and commercial boost to the city. The area to the east of the old city walls became increasingly important commercially. The development of the Grand Parade, the South Mall, and the streets running off St Patrick's Street, which were much wider and more suitable for commercial development than the narrow lanes adjoining the Main Street, all helped to shift the commercial centre of the city to the east of the areas around the Main Street. St Patrick's Street was the natural centre of this development. *(Credit: www.corkpastandpresent.ie/places/ stpatricksstreet/historicoutline/;* London Illustrated News; *Cork Library)*

TURKISH BATHS

THE GRENVILLE PLACE Turkish Baths were the first to be built by Dr Richard Barter after those at St Ann's Hydropathic Establishment at Blarney. This photograph of the baths is from the Lawrence Collection of 40,000 glass-plate negatives taken between 1870 and 1914, so it shows

the baths after the rebuilding, which took place in 1863.

It is not known how much rebuilding was actually undertaken, but if, as seems most likely, the rebuilding was only of the inside – the baths themselves – then the façade in the photograph is probably the original one.

It is interesting to note that, perhaps influenced by his nephew's fact-finding visit to Rome, Barter's building sports a classical portico rather than ogee windows and fake minarets. Clearly visible at the front of the building are the separate doors for males (on the left) and females (on the right).* *(Credit: www. victorianturkishbath.org/6DIRECTORY/ AtoZEstab/Ireland/aapix/CorkGren_w. htm. * Information about the entrances is from an advertisement for the baths which appeared in the Cork Examiner on 1 July 1859.)*

CITY HALL

ONE OF THE most splendid buildings of Cork is its City Hall, a limestone structure which replaced the old City Hall, destroyed by British troops on 11 December 1920 in a event called 'The Burning of Cork', which took place during the War of Independence. The foundation stone of the new City Hall, which was build on the site of the old building, was laid by the Executive Council of the State, Mr de Valera, on 9 July 1932.

The complete cost of this new building was provided by the British Government in the 1930s as a gesture of reconciliation. The City Hall consists of three sections: two wings comprising the Municipal Offices and an assembly hall, capable of seating up to 1,300 people. In March 1935 the first staff members of a few departments of the city administration moved into the western

wing of the building. The first council meeting was held in City Hall on 24 April 1935. The building was then officially opened by the Irish President on 8 September 1936.

Cork City is an important European example of Georgian architecture and therefore Cork City Hall was designed and built in a similar style. It is an imposing and dignified structure and, with its long main front dominating the river, immediately attracts attention due to the excellence of its proportion and the simplicity of its treatment.

The façades are of dressed limestone from the Little Island Quarries. The main entrance to the offices is through a marble-paved vestibule leading to the main staircase. The stairs are of polished marble, and the balustrade of ornamentally hammered wrought iron.

On the first floor over the entrance are the principal departments which form the Lord Mayor's suite. The Council Chamber on the opposite side of the corridor is approached through a lobby. It is well designed, being both lofty and spacious, and it receives natural light from an ornamental dome. Galleries have been provided for distinguished visitors and the general public. Here much freedom has been displayed both in the decorative and plaster work and in the balustrade, with the walls being panelled in mahogany. The furniture of the council chamber is also of mahogany, made to the architect's

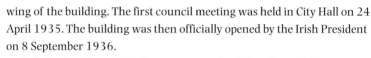

specifications.

Cork City Hall houses the office of Mayor Councillor Michael Ahern, who was elected Lord Mayor of Cork at the Annual Meeting of Cork City Council on 26 June 2006. *(Credit: Cork City Libraries, 'Cork City Hall, a Gesture of Reconciliation by the British' by Gregor Gosciniak)*

CHRISTIAN BROTHERS' SULLIVAN'S QUAY SCHOOL

THE ROOTS OF Sully's Quay are deeply embedded in Cork's oldest parish since it was opened as the Christian Brothers' second school in the city in 1828.

A few decades earlier, in 1791, the Charitable Society had been formed by a group of rich businessmen in Cork with the aim of 'providing instruction, free school requisites, clothing and employment for poor Catholic children'. Evening schools based on the so-called Lancaster model of education opened in the city in 1806 and when the then Bishop, Most Revd Dr Moylan, visited Edmund Rice in Mount Sion in 1809, the foundations were laid for the establishment of the Christian Brothers – known prior to papal approval as the Gentlemen of the Monastery – in the city.

The Brothers had begun their mission at Mount Sion, Waterford, in 1804 and their first school in the Cork area was an old cottage at Chapel Lane, near the North Cathedral, which opened its doors on 9 November 1811. A few years later, work began on a new school building at Peacock Lane; completed by the summer of 1818, it became the North Mon.

In 1827, Dean Collins asked the Christian Brothers to set up a similar school in the South Parish. A site was chosen on Sullivan's Quay and while building work was being completed, classes took place in an old store loft in Cove Street.

Sully's Quay and Deerpark (Coláiste Iognáid Ris, opened in 1968) operated hand in hand and flourished for decades, and it wasn't until the late 1970s that a decline in numbers began to be experienced. Changes in society saw young couples moving further and further away from the city centre to live, and areas near the county bounds – which had always yielded pupils for the primary school – now had schools being built locally.

Pleas for more family homes to built in the South Parish fell on deaf ears and in 2006 Sullivan's Quay CBS and South Presentation Primary School closed. *(Credit: 'Evolution' by Roger Herlihy and Michael Finn)*

THE CIRCUIT
COURTHOUSE

THIS DETACHED SEVEN-BAY, three-storey, neo-Classical courthouse was designed by James and George Richard Pain and built around 1835. The façade includes an octastyle unfluted Corinthian portico and flanking recessed outer bays articulated by Corinthian pilasters. A copper dome behind a parapet crowns the building; subsidiary double-pitched slate roofs are set between the main blocks. The walls are of ashlar limestone, with molded sills on brackets below square-headed window openings containing timber sash windows. The interior and subsidiary façades were altered in 1891.

Courtrooms 1 and 2 have timber panelling to door height around three sides. They retain the original timber seating with leather upholstery; timber panelled doors with timber moulding and architrave, some with timber pediments; a timber balcony with cast-iron Ionic columns; a coved and compartmented timber ceiling with a skylight; segmental-headed windows in square-headed window openings; a side-hung timber casement facing inward, with timber sashes facing outward. The walls are painted and nap-rendered. The bar room, connecting courtrooms 1 and 2, contains timber seating and wainscoting, panelled doors, a coved timber ceiling with skylight, a fireplace with framed mirror above, and timber sash windows.

The entrance foyer has an open arcade with marble pilasters and marble piers at ground- and first-floor levels. Timber stairs with timber balusters lead to the upper boors. Each floor is articulated by an order: Doric pilasters on the ground floor, Corinthian on the first floor, and Ionic on the second. A plaque over the entrance in the foyer commemorates the building of the interior.

CUSTOM HOUSE

THE CUSTOM HOUSE was built in 1818 and was designed by the architect Abraham Hargrave. In 1882 it became the headquarters of the Cork Harbour Commissioners, now known as the Port of Cork Company. Its elegant boardroom, where the meetings of the members of the company are held, was constructed in 1906. The old Custom House in Emmet Place is now part of the complex of buildings which houses the Crawford Municipal Art Gallery. *(Credit: www. corkpastandpresent.ie/mapsimages/corkphotographs/corkcameraclubhistoricalphotos/customhouse/)*

CHETWYND VIADUCT

THE CHETWYND VIADUCT carried the line of the West Cork Railway over a valley and the main Bandon road (now the N71) about 2 miles (3km) south-west of Cork City. It was designed by Charles Nixon (a former pupil of I.K. Brunel) and built between 1849 and 1851 by Fox, Henderson & Co., who also built the Crystal Palace in London. It was in use until the line was closed in 1961.

The viaduct is 91ft (28m) high and has four 110ft (34m) spans, each span composed of four cast-iron arched ribs, carried on masonry piers 20ft (6m) thick and 30ft (9m) wide. The overall span between end abutments is 500ft (150m).

The 100ft (30m) cast-iron ribs were cast on site. When in situ they had transverse diagonal bracing and lattice spandrels that supported a deck of iron plates. These in turn supported the permanent way.

The structure was seriously damaged in the Irish Civil War in 1922, but was subsequently repaired. To this day, the Chetwynd Viaduct still straddles the Cork–Bandon road, although the last

train to pass over was on 31 March 1961, when the West Cork Railway officially closed.

The viaduct was the 'Everest' of road bowling and was conquered after decades of attempts, on 8 September 1985. Watched by over 10,000 people, Hans Bohllen from West Germany lofted a 28oz bowl over the viaduct, clearing the top by 10ft.

The event was sponsored by Murphy's Brewery Ireland in association with Bol-Chumann Na hÉireann as part of the Cork 800 Celebrations. Hans Bohllen received a prize of £5,000.

Three Irish bowlers (all Cork based), Bill Daly, Eamonn Bowen and Dan O'Halloran also successfully lofted the viaduct with the 16oz bowl and shared another Murphy prize of £1,000.

Dr George Reilly, then a lecturer in mathematical physics in University College, Cork was asked by *Cork Examiner* journalist Val Dorgan to give a theoretic account of what it would be to loft the Chetwynd Viaduct. Dr Reilly said that to get a 28oz bowl over the viaduct, one must stand back about 45ft, pitch it at an angle of 77 degrees and give the bowl a velocity of at least 20ft per second. *(Credit: www.wikipedia.org/wiki/Cork,_Bandon_and_South_Coast_Railway and www.askaboutireland.ie/reading-room/sports-recreation/sport/road-bowling/chetwynd-viaduct/)*

TITANIC

THE SINKING OF *Titanic* caused the deaths of 1,517 people, making it one of the deadliest peacetime maritime disasters in history. She was the largest ship afloat at the time of her maiden voyage. The disaster was greeted with worldwide shock and outrage at the huge loss of life and the regulatory and operational failures that had led to it. Public inquiries in Britain and the United States led to major improvements in maritime safety.

Titanic had left Southampton on her maiden voyage on 10 April 1912, and after a first stop in Cherbourg, France, she proceeded to Queenstown, Ireland, where she arrived on 11 April.

Known today as Cobh, Queenstown did not have a dock big enough for the massive ship. Frank Browne, 2nd officer David Blair and other passengers and goods were transported to and from shore on a tender named *America*. Launch tickets were used whenever people and baggage were ferried in this fashion.

The price of a ticket for *Titanic*'s maiden voyage varied greatly depending on class. The range was $4,350 for first class (capacity 905) to $30 for steerage passage (capacity 1,134). Second-class accommodations (capacity 564) were $1,750. When the ship left Queenstown she had 2,200 souls aboard, including crew.

Many passengers travelled with a great deal of luggage. They received baggage coupons and excess luggage tickets for each piece. The total amount of passenger luggage, however, paled when compared to the total provisions *Titanic* carried on her maiden voyage. From 8,000 cigars to 75,000lbs of fresh meat – and 40 tons of potatoes – no one would go hungry while the ship was at sea. First-class passengers would be hard-pressed to enjoy better dinners on land.

As she weighed anchor for the last time, *Titanic* left Queenstown on 11 April. *(Text credit: www.wikipedia.org/wiki/Titanic. Photo credit: Davison and Associates Ltd, Dublin www.Davisonphoto.com)*

CHRISTCHURCH

CHRISTCHURCH, ALSO KNOWN as the Holy Trinity, is located on South Main Street, once the main street of medieval Cork. Christchurch ceased to function as a place of worship (Church of Ireland) in 1978 before the building was acquired by Cork City Council the following year to house the Cork Archives Institute, where they resided before relocating to new purpose-built premises in Blackpool in 2005. In 2008, a €4.8 million refurbishment project was undertaken by Cork City Council, who applied for and were successful in obtaining €2.18 million of funding from the EU Structural Funds 2007-20 13, the European Regional Development Fund, and the Southern and Eastern Regional Assembly. Triskel Arts Centre manages the building on behalf of Cork City Council and has developed Christchurch into a cultural and artistic hub for the city.

Present-day Christchurch is an eighteenth-century neoclassical Georgian building (1718-1726) designed by Cork architect John Coltsman, who also designed the North and South Gate Bridges (the South Gate Bridge has one of the oldest surviving three-centred arches in Ireland). In 1825, the façade of Christchurch was redesigned by George Richard Pain, who was later involved in remodelling the interior. The church sits on the site of two previous churches dating back to medieval times. It is suggested that the original building of Christchurch took place around 1050 and was of Hiberno-Norse or Viking origin, and that it also may have been the first church built in the city. Christchurch was in the hub of the town captured and colonised by the Anglo-Normans in 1177 and in 1180 they rebuilt Christchurch as a stone structure. There is evidence suggesting that at least two side-chapels existed at Christchurch; an eighteenth-century Lady chapel to the north and a sixteenth-century chapel dedicated to St James to the south. Little is known about the chapels or the medieval church, as nothing remains of the pre-1700 fabric of the church with the possible exception of part of the crypt.

Early documentary evidence for Christchurch comes from the year 1199, when Pope Innocent III refers to it in his Decretal Letter. Christchurch was the primary location where city officials would gather on all festive and important occasions and it was the burial place of some of the chief citizens of Cork, with names such as Terry, Skyddy, Roche and Ronan. The most well-known tombstone within Christchurch is that of Thomas Ronan, who was Mayor of Cork in 1537 and again in 1549. Ronan died in 1554 and he is buried with his wife Johanna Tyrry. The tombstone, commonly referred to as 'The Modest Man', is visible in the porch entrance to Christchurch. *(Credit: Triskel Arts Cewntre, Cork)*

MARINA

MUCH OF THE land on the south bank of the Lee from the City Hall to Blackrock Castle is reclaimed slobland. In the 1760s, Cork Corporation began the construction of the Navigation Wall, which was also called the New Wall. The Navigation Wall was built to prevent the silting up of the river channel with mud. By the middle of the nineteenth century, Cork Harbour Commissioners began dredging the south slobland to allow larger ships, with a greater draught of water, access to the city quay. The dredged-up material was deposited behind the Navigation Wall. This deposit of compacted mud and silt eventually formed the Marina. When the promenade had been completed in 1870, the Gaelic poet and scholar Donncha Ó Floinn suggested to the Improvements Committee of Cork Corporation that it be named Slí na hAbhann, which means the 'pathway by the river'. Ó Floinn's proposal was defeated. The matter came before the Improvements Committee again in 1872. This time Ó Floinn suggested that the promenade be named 'The Marina'. He pointed out that 'The Marina' was the name given to recently reclaimed land near Palermo in Sicily. In July 1872, Cork Corporation formally adopted 'The Marina' as the name of the new promenade.

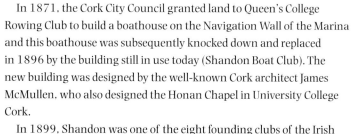

In 1871, the Cork City Council granted land to Queen's College Rowing Club to build a boathouse on the Navigation Wall of the Marina and this boathouse was subsequently knocked down and replaced in 1896 by the building still in use today (Shandon Boat Club). The new building was designed by the well-known Cork architect James McMullen, who also designed the Honan Chapel in University College Cork.

In 1899, Shandon was one of the eight founding clubs of the Irish Amateur Rowing Union. In 1902 'The International Cup Races' were held at Cork, marking the climax of the great Cork Exhibition of that summer. The regatta was the greatest rowing carnival ever held in Ireland and the final day was attended by an estimated 80,000 spectators. Shandon was one of thirteen clubs to enter a crew in the race for senior eights in which Leander of London beat Berlin Rowing Club in the final.

In 1917, a Ford Motors assembly plant was established in Cork beside the Shandon Boat Club. This resulted in the subsequent closing off of the Marina from the city centre. *(Credit: www.shandonboatclub. com/about-sbc/history.html and www.askaboutireland.ie/reading-room/ history-heritage/architecture/the-cork-camera-club-(pre/the-quays/ marinavictoria-quay/)*

THE MANGAN CLOCK

THE MANGAN CLOCK has been a landmark on St Patrick's Street since the 1850s. Mangan Jewellers, founded in 1817 and formerly one of the best-known shops on the street, erected the clock. In 1847, craftsmen at Mangan's built the four-faced clock on Shandon church steeple. This was reputed to be the largest four-faced clock in the world, until the construction of the clock tower of Big Ben in London.

Mangan's shop narrowly escaped destruction in December 1920 when a British auxiliary threw a grenade into the premises, intending to ignite

a can of petrol which he had placed there. The petrol did not catch fire but the grenade blew out all the windows of the shop. Mangan's shop ceased trading in the late 1980s, before the premises were demolished, along with many others, to allow for the construction of the Merchant's Quay Shopping Centre. The Mangan Clock, on its tall kerbside pedestal, has been incorporated into the recent refurbishment of St Patrick's Street. *(Credit: www.corkpastandpresent.ie/places/ stpatricksstreet/selectedplacesofinterest/manganjewellersmangansclock/)*

If you enjoyed this book, you may also be interested in ...

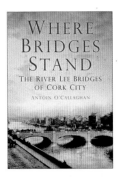

Where Bridges Stand

ANTÓIN O'CALLAGHAN

Where Bridges Stand: The River Lee Bridges of Cork City tells the story of how the city grew around, and in harmony with, the bridges that span the twin channels of the River Lee, and the people and the historical contexts associated with the building projects that saw Cork grow from a medieval walled town to the thriving modern city that it is today.

978 1 84588 746 9

Haunted Cork

DARREN MANN

Featuring stories of unexplained phenomena, apparitions, poltergeists, changelings and banshees, and including accounts of mysterious vanishing islands, ghosts of shipwrecked Spanish sailors, and, of course, the story behind the legendary Blarney Stone, *Haunted Cork* contains many spooky narratives that are guaranteed to make your blood run cold.

978 1 84588 694 3

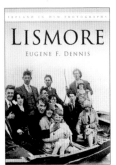

Lismore In Old Photographs

EUGENE F. DENNIS

Lismore has, without doubt, a fascinating history, and is widely regarded as Waterford's most historic town. This diverse collection of rare archive images captures the changes in Lismore's industry, transport and schools as well as recording its sporting achievements, art in the parish and, of course, its inhabitants, producing a timeless volume that will enthral all those who know and love the area.

978 1 84588 690 5

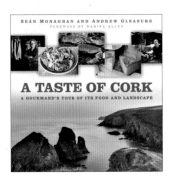

A Taste of Cork

SEÁN MONAGHAN & ANDREW GLEASURE

In this book, one of Ireland's top photographers, Seán Monaghan, presents Cork's rich and diverse landscape in a new light, combining the spectacular vistas with the world of the artisan gourmet food producers who are so much a part of the culture. Seán Monaghan describes the motivations and method behind his photographs, while Andrew Gleasure recounts the anecdotes and individual stories of the people.

978 1 84588 714 8

Visit our website and discover thousands of other History Press books.

www.thehistorypress.ie